Jasmine

Rajah

Genie

Abu and the
Magic Carpet

Sultan

Jafar
and Iago

Aladdin was so hungry, he stole some bread.

"Stop, thief!"

"Someday, I'll live in a palace, Abu."

Princess Jasmine and her pet tiger, Rajah

"I don't want to be a princess anymore," said Jasmine.

"I know! I'll disguise myself and run away!"

Jasmine took an apple to give to a hungry boy.

"You stole an apple, you thief!" cried a market guard.

Aladdin rescued Jasmine from the guards.

Jafar must find out who has Princess Jasmine.

Aladdin was taken to the palace dungeon.

Jafar (disguised as an old man) freed Aladdin
and led him through the desert.

Only a "Diamond in the Rough" can enter...

...the Cave of Wonders!

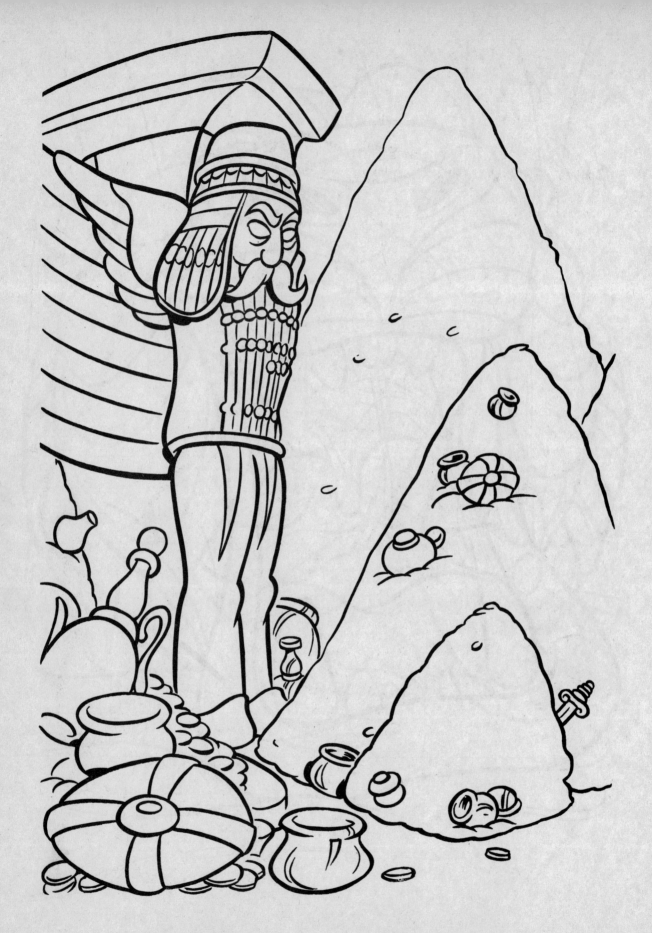

Aladdin and Abu saw amazing treasures!

Aladdin found a lamp!

What power does the lamp have?

Out of the lamp came... a Genie!

"You may have three wishes!"

"I wish to be a prince!" said Aladdin.

Abu became an elephant.

Aladdin flew off to find Jasmine.

Aladdin showed Jasmine an amazing world.

Jasmine knew she had found her prince.

Wishes do come true!

Young Tarzan grew up in the jungle.

The animals took care of Tarzan.

Tarzan's best friends were Terk and Tantor.

Tarzan and Terk made a great team!

Tarzan learned to swing on the jungle vines.

By the time he grew up,
he could practically fly through the jungle!

Tarzan met the professor's daughter, Jane.

Tarzan was a hero! He rescued Jane
from danger, and they fell in love.

Robin Hood was the hero of Nottingham!

He and his band of Merry Men
stole from the rich and gave to the poor.

Little John was a faithful friend.

Prince John was rich and greedy.

He was always plotting to
collect more taxes from the poor!

"Our disguises will fool Prince John."

"Isn't it unlawful to rob a prince?"

"Robin Hood is sure fooling that prince."

"Stop them!"

Crafty Robin Hood foiled Prince John's plans.

"There's to be an Archery Tournament tomorrow."

"Maid Marian will surely be there."

"Nobody will know me in this stork outfit."

"I shall go as Sir Reginald the Duke of Chutney."

"Wish me well, Lady Marian!"

"Good luck, friend Archer!"

"Seize this imposter!"

The Merry Men fought Prince John's guards.

Robin Hood rescued the fair Maid Marian.

The good folk of Nottingham made off with the gold!

It's all in a day's work—for heroes!

Peter is a very clever boy!

"Look, Wendy! Never Land!"

"We'll have wonderful adventures together."

"Peter Pan! Ahoy!"

"Swoogle me eyes! He'll not win again!"

"Fire away, me mateys!"

But Peter Pan and Tinker Bell are safe.

What is Captain Hook up to?

He has captured the Indian Princess, Tiger Lily!

© 2008 Disney

"I'll rescue Tiger Lily," vows Peter.

Hook is left to the Crocodile!

Peter Pan is a hero!

The Chief thanks Peter Pan.

The mermaids aren't nice to Wendy.

Peter banishes Tinker Bell for being mean to Wendy, too.

"Tell me where Peter Pan's hideout is," says Captain Hook.

Hook promises not to hurt Peter.

Will Tinker Bell reveal Peter's hiding place?
Yes!

Hook tricks Tinker Bell into helping him.

"I know how we'll lead Peter Pan to us," says Hook.

"We'll capture Wendy!"

Will the children all become pirates?

"Never!" insists Wendy.

Wendy must walk the plank...

...but Peter Pan rescues her!

Will Captain Hook defeat Peter Pan?

The loser is... Captain Hook!

Peter Pan is Captain of the ship!

"Thank you for rescuing us, Peter."

The ship sails through the sky...

...back home to London.

Farewell, Peter Pan!